Knitting 20th Century Art

Dedication

For Dad, who carried me out to the window, who held me when I was sick, who was the best father he could be.

Acknowledgments

In all my life endeavors, I depend on the support of others. Nothing of value is accomplished alone, in a vacuum of solitude. This is most true when it comes to giving birth to a book. I owe a debt of gratitude to people, both living and dead. The artists—the painters—who unwittingly encouraged my own artistic expression have long-since passed away. Still, I thank them for their art. To my grandmother who gave me the gift of knitting and to my Dad, from whom I inherited the desire to create, I thank you both and miss you every day. To my living, loving friends I also owe this debt of gratitude. To Petra Vatne, your at-the-ready photography expertise and friendship are treasured by me. Thank you. To Jeanette Gingold, my friend who keeps me rooted, your common sense, don't-overthink-things counsel and your honest feedback are priceless. Thank you for your constant willingness to help, to edit, and to critique. Last but by no means least, thank you for the perfect book title. To Marjorie Anderson, thank you for your dissertation-level research on my behalf, for your editing acumen, for your memory and for your nerdy sense of humor. You are a woman after my own heart. To the models Jillian, Stacy, Carrina, Natascha, Solange , Rena and Audrey, thank you for making my projects beautiful. To Joan, I so very much appreciate your knowledge of, and experience in, the art world. Thank you for your ideas and your willingness to share your expertise with me. To all of my Gab 'n' Knit friends, thank you for your interest in my work and for your support. Likewise my friends on Ravelry and in my group, Colorworks by Debi, your faith in my ability to design and write books is something I struggle to live up to. Thank you for being with me every day via the Internet. And to my Andrew, thank you for learning to be a techie where I cannot.

Thank you for nagging me into making this the best project it can be. You know I am lazy and the book would have been much less without you pushing me. Thank you for jumping up and coming to my rescue almost every time I hollered, which was quite often. I love you.

Foreword

All of the human arts exist within one relentless, lava-like flow that meanders through the ages. However, styles change over time, and those changes take place almost imperceptibly. When we compare the arts at one moment to those of another era, we find wide divergence. It's sometimes hard to see these differences and to discuss the arts unless we place an artificial grid over our rather amorphous perception. This grid is a terminology, a logical vocabulary, that we employ when discuss our sensory experience. This linguistic verbal structure helps us to distinguish one style from another or the type of work produced in one location from the work done in another and helps organize our thoughts. For ease of analysis and for understanding, specialists group particular arts into schools or movements in which certain stylistic features are common to those working in a given time and place. The glazed pottery known as Delftware or woodworking associated with the Shaker communities, for example, are two stylistic schools that many of us have some knowledge of. It doesn't matter who created the works. The works themselves are identifiable and classified, rather than the work of individual crafters.

Similarities in personal and cultural style and techniques make groups of artist cohere. Usually, in the so-called high culture of Western Europe, scholars divide the big sweep of artistic expression into historical style periods. Most of us might be familiar with the "Renaissance" or perhaps the "Victorian Era," terms that mark two periods in which a kind of worldview grows out of the knowledge, philosophy, technology and politics of an epoch as a more-or-less unified concept of a way of life. In art, this worldview is called aesthetics. Aesthetics can be simply defined as "the theory of the beautiful." However it's more complicated than that. Aesthetics is the realization and articulation of the fact that works of art have emotional effects on humans.

Modernism is a historical style period that has roots back in the 19th century. The composer Richard Wagner, in a mid-century letter to Franz Liszt wrote, "Children, make new things and new again!" This idea echoed across the years and became a rallying cry for creative spirits in the arts everywhere. In part, aesthetics of the time were becoming confused with technology and science and with the great leaps forward made during the Industrial Revolution. Life became better for people as time marched on, therefore the future promised unimagined devices and conveniences to alleviate the drudgery of daily existence. Artists, likewise, became obsessed with the future. They began to question whether their art was bound to its own time period or whether their purpose was to create art for future generations as they believed artisans and architects of ages past created great monuments for their enjoyment.

The new styles that developed from these ideas first started to be felt in the 20th century, before the First World War. Many of the artistic movements in both the visual arts and music rejected the rather emotional, literary-based representations of reality that were part of the 19th-century period commonly known as Romanticism. The aesthetics of the new century reflected an appreciation of the intellectual, the non-referential, and the abstract expression of the solitary, heroic artist. In a world that was completely overwhelmed by the image-creation of not only a photography popularized by Kodak, but also a growing cinema industry, the drive toward a painterly expression of the real world waned. Painting became less the act of representation of a historical moment than a "painting" *per se*. The arts were understood, not so much as storytelling devices, but as arrangements of color, line, shape (through visual media) and sounds (music). A painting, for example, became nothing more than a painting, but nothing less as well.

The impulse toward newness was also accompanied by a series of theoretical frameworks that the artists themselves constructed so that they could position their aesthetic expression within a greater world of ideas. As each school of Modernism developed, it engendered a spate of words, and often, manifestos or formal statements of purpose. This might seem odd to us today, strange that art would need some type of justification. However, art that had moved from visual storytelling to purely intellectual activity was certainly aided by some accompanying verbal explanation.

Each school and sub-movement developed from a previous one, and the aesthetics propelled art continually to invent and re-invent different manifestations of itself. It is as if Wagner's call to make things "new again" permeated all the arts. So what we witness is a plethora of styles, many of them similar to others, but which, for one reason or another, were finely delineated from their precursors or from other movements. The long list of Modernist styles in literature, art and music is mindboggling. Nonetheless there are several that almost all of us have heard of and a few with which many of us are familiar, if only in a cursory way.

Art was seemingly mimicking technology and adopting the "newness means progress" and "the future will be better than the past" world view, aesthetic ideas that we might see today as wrongheaded. A great painting, say, Picasso's *Guernica*, is different from—not better than—Leonardo's *Mona Lisa*. That is not to say that all works of art are of the same quality, but the very novelty of a work neither makes it necessarily better than something from the past nor does it allow us to relegate art from the past to the ash heap of history. Modernists held themselves to be cultural supermen of a sort and pooh-poohed any rejection of their works as *too* difficult or as alienating to the general public.

However, what is also clear is that many Modernists produced simplified works or works that were practical, enjoyed by the masses, and socially quite acceptable. The composer Aaron Copland, for example, wrote several film scores and perhaps today is still most well-known for his *Fanfare for the Common Man*. Many fine artists acted as illustrators or were employed as muralists for public spaces. Simplified design elements from Modernism entered into advertising and were incorporated into objects for daily use, like furniture, lighting, and household appliances. Eventually, ideas that seemed theoretical and quite out-of-the ordinary at the beginning of the century became commonplace. Designs once thought too bold and shocking were found everywhere.

As the Modernist period began to come to an end with the work of the Pop artists, the world started to see a return to simple representation, to forms and subjects that seemed—for lack of a better term—"traditional," and sometimes to the reworking of material of artists of previous generations. And that's where we find ourselves today: in a world that is post-Modern. Whereas popular and folk arts were once considered beneath the high art of Modernism, today all media, all styles, and all creative activity is *prima facie* accorded the respect of scholars and critics. In our period, eclecticism, appropriation and repurposing, mash-up and parody are part of all the arts, from the visual—including film and television—to literature and music—including rap and electronic dance music (EDM). So this book is a kind of postmodern appropriation of Modernist themes, a collage of ideas of the 20th century not expressed in the media of the so-called high arts. It offers a folk-like pastiche of home craft and fine art from the museum, ironic at times but in all cases thoughtful.

Modernism, however, was nothing if not original. In its practicality and simplicity of design, Modernism has left its indelible mark on the century in which most of us were born, and we find these traces today in our cities, in our homes, and in all things designed. And it is in deference to this Modernism and its great artists that this book appears.

—Andrew Tomasello

Preface

I wrote *Knitting 20th-Century Art* for people, like me, whose knowledge of art history would fit neatly on the tip of a knitting needle. With room to spare. It is a humorous approach to the topic that informs a little, but encourages a lot— a lot of giggles. It's a loose-knit survey of 20th-century art movements, if you will. The ten patterns included were inspired by recognizable art styles from the last 110 years or so. What I deem as silly when hanging in oils on a wall, I find stunning when knitted into a garment or accessory and hanging on a person. But, this book will also appeal to art history buffs, as it will expose them to the idiocy and ignorance of their lessers. The text will prove be irresistibly amusing. And the knitted pieces, for art aficionados, will have an intrinsically deeper meaning.

I cover an important topic heretofore overlooked in knitting books. When working to achieve knitting nirvana, we knitters need to own our imperfections. Mistakes are allowed. Sometimes they are okay. It is my contention (with no support whatsoever beyond experience) that many wonderful stitches were inadvertently created. That is to say they were born as mistakes. This is easy to imagine with the "mistake rib" stitch. Likewise, we all made holes when we started knitting. Now, we make them on purpose and we call them lace. The Mobius Cowl? Someone twisted her stitches and decided to go with it. A miracle was born! Fortunate accidents they are, but blunders nonetheless. We are not perfect, and our art reflects that, whether we like it or not. So, we need to relax about the idea of perfection in our work. Being okay with imperfection aids in making knitting the joy it should be. I aim to make the idea of tinking history, or at least extremely rare.

In *Knitting 20th Century Art*, I explain what colorwork is, the choices involved before beginning a project, and the importance of maintaining an even tension and floats when stranding. I also discuss how to read colorwork charts and how these differ from other knitting charts. I include links to the helpful visuals available via YouTube.

I have included patterns for socks, hats, mitts, shawls, a cowl, a felted bag and a sweater: ten patterns total. The collection comprises patterns employing the stranded knitting and intarsia techniques, which are explained in the text. One pattern encourages embroidery or needlepoint embellishments. Some beads can be used as well as duplicate stitching. Hence, there is something within these pages to appeal to knitters of all stripes.

Contents

Introduction

Color is the perception of light waves as they reflect off objects. The normal visual spectrum of wavelengths is limited, in humans, to those between approximately 390 nm* and 700 nm.

We knitters love color. And that love for color can be most fully exploited when we knit colorwork, be it stranding, intarsia, slip-stitch, or embroidering. My favorite colorwork method is stranding and, for the most part, stranding is the method that I most often use in the following patterns. However, I do have a pattern that employs intarsia (*Mondrianesque,* pg. 38). And I have a felted pattern that uses embellishing (*Remembering Cubism: The Felted Bag,* pg. 45). I will fully explain all techniques used.

I have often said, and it has become the quote that I regularly use in my bios,

> **Some people see a gorgeous sunset and photograph it. Others paint it. I knit it. Fiber and fabric are my media. Knitting that sunset makes it mine.**

That sunset can be knitted in an infinite number of ways. It's up to the interpretation and desires of the artist. (And yes, knitting is an art.) I use color to best describe my ideas, and stranding, for me, is the best way to employ color. If I were to knit my *Snowflake Stranded Shawl,* for example in hot pink and orange, I would convey a completely different mood from the chilly anticipation of winter that comes across with the ice blue and white yarn I used. You get the point.

*Nanometer—a unit of length in the metric system, equal to one billionth of a meter

Here, I bring together several of my colorwork designs that were inspired by artists who painted. And, I have added one or two designs that simply reflect the mood of a decade (*i.e., Groovy! The Socks,* pg. 58) Mine are not copies of the great works, but they are a nod to the brilliance of the artists and a reflection of my admiration for the colors and themes they chose. Some are quirky, some are elegant, and some are plain ol' fun. My hope is that you will enjoy knitting them as much as I did. Remember, YOU are the artist. The palette is in YOUR hands. You may interpret and color your pieces as you will. Use the yarns and colors I suggest, or feel free to change them up and do your own thing.

From the research I did for the writing of this book, I found, and this should not have come as a surprise, that art movements are completely entwined in the politics of the day. In order to more thoroughly understand a given art movement, one must delve into a study of history, of prevailing, time-appropriate culture, of attitudes and counter-attitudes of a people. To call my background an "overview" is misleading. Mine is a surface swipe, a general mini-description of the movements that inspired my work. I am not an art historian. But, obviously, I am influenced by art, as we all are, either directly or indirectly. We can appreciate works simply for their beauty. Knowing the hows, whens and whys behind a piece can only serve to deepen that appreciation. Unless otherwise stated, my research was conveniently confined to the wonderful information in Wikipedia.

We knitters are artists. We pick up needles in lieu of brushes, and palettes of yarn become our paints. Our canvas is our imagination. And, our work is important.

I had a husband once who used to like to shop for tools. We'd be milling about in Sears, and I'd be happy as the proverbial clam, shopping for housewares and linens. But when we'd wander into the tool department, a sudden lethargy and boredom would sweep over me, and I'd have an urgent desire to be unconscious. I once complained to the customer service guy because they offered no chairs in that department for bored and weary me. Anyway, I told you that by way of explaining what art history study does to me. I glaze over. Far too many unknowns and whole bunches of I don't really cares.

When it comes to art, I know what I like. That's about it. I know a few names. I know Picasso did something called Cubism. I think it's weird-looking, but it makes for great knitting fun. I know of Dalí and his funny-looking slippery, melting clocks. I don't get the *why* of the work. I just giggle when I see it. And I picture a floppy tam. So, I designed one. What makes me giggle hanging on the wall makes me ooh and ah when worn on my head. Go figure.

Art history? Yawn! Knitting art? Yay!

Abbreviations

BO — bind off

CO — cast on

DPN — double-pointed needle

Dec — decrease

Inc — increase

K — knit

K2TOG — knit two stitches together

M1 — knit in front loop and then again in the back loop of stitch

MC — main color

PM — place marker

P — purl

Rnd — round

SSK — slip one stitch, then slip the next. Insert left needle into the front loops of the slipped stitches and knit them together from this position

Colorwork Techniques I Use

Stranding: Most of the patterns in this book use the stranded technique. And, because stranding can be accomplished almost exclusively in-the-round (as opposed to flat, or back and forth), the knitter can avoid purling, for the most part. You certainly can strand "flat," or back and forth. But, you don't have to. A colorwork chart can be read to accommodate either flat or in-the-round. If you strand the piece flat, you read, generally, odd-numbered rows from right to left and even-numbered rows from left to right. The side of the chart on which the row number appears is the side from which you begin working that row. Most of us have referred to the stranded method as Fair Isle, but there is a slight distinction. Fair Isle is named after designs emanating from an island by that name, which is north of Scotland and is one of the Shetland Islands. But Fair Isle only uses two strands of yarn in a given round and has a limited palette of very few colors. Stranded rounds, by contrast, can comprise two, three or even four color strands per round, and the color possibilities are only as limited as the knitter's imagination. In short, while all Fair Isle is stranded, not all stranded is Fair Isle.

Traditionally, rules have existed for the "proper" way to hold yarns while stranding. We have the *Portuguese* method where the knitter holds her yarns around her neck. The yarn is sometimes placed in a pin on her lapel. This practice frees up her hands, gives relief to that poor index finger used for tensioning in Continental knitting, and yarn tension issues are taken care of almost unconsciously. The technique also helps prevent the yarns from tangling. We also have the *Continental* method where the knitter holds her dominant yarn in one hand and her background yarn in the other. She scoops the yarn she wants for a given stitch, as needed. Also, we have the practice of holding both yarns in one hand, called *One-hand* stranding. For knitters, like me, who are throwers, this method works best. By simply picking up the desired strand, knitting as needed, dropping it and grabbing the other strand, we accomplish our colorwork designs.

There are no right-or-wrong rules when it comes to holding your yarn. Do what works for you. If you can accomplish a piece that looks as nice on the back as it does on the front, you are doing it correctly. Practice, and you will find a method that is comfortable for you. Most important is to find a way that makes stranding the joy it should be.

Intarsia: Intarsia is a technique wherein fields of different colors, which seem to be inlaid in one another, are merely separate pieces worked together as you go like pieces of a jigsaw puzzle. Unlike alternative colorwork techniques, intarsia employs the use of only one active color at a time. The unused strands of yarn are not carried across the back but are left dangling while the current color is worked. Rather than worked in the round as with other colorwork techniques, intarsia is commonly worked flat, or back and forth.

If, for example, the knitter is creating a blue square on a white background (See picture below), she will knit across the background with white yarn until she reaches the part that requires blue for the square. She will then drop the white yarn, attach or pick up the blue, knit the width of the square, then drop the blue strand and pick up or attach a white strand and continue across. For the next row, she will turn the work around, purl back across the background with the white yarn, drop it and pick up blue for her square, purl the square, drop that strand, pick up the white strand she had dropped on the previous row and continue across purling the background white. This method works well for objects that require large areas of solid colors. It is the method used for knitting *Mondrianesque*, the sweater pattern included in this book. (pg. 38)

Embellishment: Sometimes we want to add a little extra something of interest to our piece, be it beads, duplicate stitches, embroidery, buttons or anything else our creative minds imagine. These added design elements are called embellishments. Many of my patterns allow for embellishments. A note of caution is needed here, though. If a colorwork design is already busy, adding embellishments might clutter and actually distract from, rather than add to, the beauty of a piece. So, the knitter is wise to take care when considering such additions. Two of the patterns I am including in the book call for embellishments: *Autumn Rhythm: the Fingerless Mitts*, (pg.66) and *Remembering Cubism: The Felted Bag*, (pg.45). The mitts, because they were inspired by Jackson Pollock's work, scream for thoughtfully placed duplicate stitches or embroidery. The felted bag, itself, is solid black. The Cubism design is added by embroidering it, duplicate-stitching it, or needlepointing on canvas and then attaching. I used needlepoint. You can add the design whichever way appeals to you.

Helpful Tutorials

Reading Colorwork Charts: Reading colorwork charts is much the same as reading other knitting charts. But there are differences. Like most charts, colorwork charts are generally read from right to left and from bottom to top. If you are working rows back and forth, the purl rows will be numbered on the left, and you work them from left to right. In short, you start working on the side of the chart where you see the row number, and you work across from that point. Each square of the chart grid represents one stitch. Like lace charts, decreases and future increases on colorwork charts are denoted by blank spaces, showing the lack of stitch where one used to be or where one will be, eventually.

Now for the major difference: Lacework chart squares are filled with symbols representing the type of stitch to be worked in that spot, and they are accompanied by legends that explain what the symbols mean. Colorwork charts are written differently. Because colorwork in the round is worked all in stockinette, the knit stitch is a given. There is no need to mark the stitch type, except occasionally when a purl stitch is required. The grid and or instructions will give directions. What the knitter does need to know is which color to work in a particular spot. So, colorwork charts have colors in the squares, rather than symbols, and color key legends where needed to describe what color stitches to make and where. See my YouTube video for instruction on reading my colorwork charts.

https://www.youtube.com/watch?v=rMyZXIsxFhw

And another: https://www.youtube.com/watch?v=NW7Un1gXRmc

Floating and Tension: Tension, in this context refers to floating uniformity, not gauge. Tension is arguably the most critical element in stranded knitting. It is vital to keep an even, consistent tension when stranding. This takes a little practice. I say "a little" practice, because it really doesn't take much. I am fond of saying, "Remember LEO when floating. Float LOOSELY, EVENLY and OFTEN." See my YouTube video for help with the concept of floating and tension. https://www.youtube.com/watch?v=jQlc4UQWuzc

A note on **Yarn Dominance**: The above video leads us to the related issue of yarn dominance, a thing I described in the tutorial without specifically naming it. Yarn dominance refers to the way you carry your yarn to produce a dominant color on the front. You noticed in my baby sweater that most of the time, I held the white yarn in the dominant, or "over" position, crossing it over the pink on the back when necessary. But, for that one knitting period, I inadvertently switched my yarns, making the pink the yarn carried in the "over" position. This changed the appearance on the front, creating an unwanted pinkish stripe in the fabric. You will want to pay attention to yarn dominance. Some designs show inconsistencies more than others, but as long as you hold the yarns in the same position each time you knit, you will avoid trouble. If you hold color A in your right hand and color B in your left…always hold them in those hands. If you get up to make a cup of coffee and come back and pick the yarns up the other way (A in your left hand and B in your right), you will have that disturbing color variation on the front. If color A is between your big toe and second toe, and color B is held by your pinky toe, keep the yarns in those toe positions throughout the project. Another, perhaps clearer example of a knitter who inadvertently ignored the yarn dominance issue is pictured below.

Lucy Neatby's Paradoxical Mittens Courtesy of Wendy Preston

Yarn Choices

I need to say a little something here about choosing yarns for colorwork projects. Much of the text below appears as it did in *Wrapped in Color: Stranded Knitting in the 21st Century*. It's reasonable that this be so because yarn information is the same now as it was then; nothing has changed. It bears restating here. An important feature of colorwork is the pattern design itself. If you want to highlight the colorwork design, you will want to use a hardtwist yarn. A hardtwist fiber will produce great stitch definition and will highlight the design the pattern intends. Hardtwist is a yarn that lacks a halo, those furry, hairy little fibers that stick out and make the yarn appear fuzzy. Although very soft and appealing, yarns like this tend to obscure the stitch pattern. On the other hand, if you want to blur or soften the design, a haloed yarn might be a choice you prefer. The edges of one color will blend with the next color, creating an effect different from, but not necessarily less appealing than, the same design worked with a hardtwist. You are the artist. The choice is yours.

Although colorwork can be worked with any weight yarn, (lace, fingering, DK, worsted, and so on), it is good to keep in mind that, when stranding, you will automatically add thickness and bulk to your piece by virtue of the fact that you are carrying the unused yarn across the back of your work. If you choose to use a heavier yarn, and you still want drape, be sure to increase the needle size. If you want a stiffer, denser fabric, use a smaller needle for a more tightly knit project.

Except for two patterns in this book that require worsted-weight yarns *Remembering Cubism: The Felted Bag* (pg. 45) and *Autumn Rhythm: The Fingerless Mitts* (pg.66), the patterns call for fingering-weight wool. I use Knit Picks Palette almost exclusively, and for a couple of reasons. First, Palette offers about 150 colors. This suits me. Second the cost is quite reasonable, which also suits me. Having said that, you may substitute any comparable yarn. Cascade 220 Fingering works well, as do a number of sock yarns. I prefer wool to cotton or acrylic. Wool works up easily, blocks better, and generally keeps its shape better than other yarns. For hats and fingering-weight wool, a #3 needle works well. For my shawls, because I want to produce a loose, fabric with lots of drape, I will use a #9 needle. Again, you are the artist, and you make the choice for your project. Work some swatches until you get the look and feel you want. Just make sure you adjust gauge so the size remains true.

Owning Your Imperfections

Knitting is pure, unadulterated joy. At least, it should be. I feel bad for knitters who get caught up in every mistake, tinking and frogging. There's an entire vocabulary built around knitting boo-boos. Some of the words are not suitable for print here. This obsession with errors, this desire to knit a flawless piece, will zap the joy out of the process. Many cultures uphold the traditional of building mistakes purposely into their work as a sign of humility. Only God or Allah is perfect is the justification. I always saw this as the opposite of humility. We must force a mistake? Isn't that like admitting that if we didn't *purposely* create an error in our design, we would be betraying our actual perfection?

I don't know about you, but I don't have to try, or even knit very far into a piece, before I prove my lack of godly perfection. But, I have found the joy in allowing myself to be less than perfect. My current rule of thumb is, if I say, "Oops, nobody will notice" more than five times, it's probably a good idea to start again. Short of that fifth time, it's ok to move forward.

Consider the lovely work of the spider pictured above. She worked tirelessly on that web, spinning and spinning. At the end of the day, when she finally sat down to contemplate her web, she looked back at the beginning, near the center, and discovered a hole. Oh no! Did she think "I have to nips back?" (Nips is the spider equivalent of tink. Tink is "knit" backward, and nips is, you got it, "spin" backward.) Of course not! She moved happily forward in her spider life. And we marvel at her web. It is gorgeous just as it is.

We do well to learn from the humble, if terrifying, spider. The joy of knitting is in the doing. It proves nothing and increases our happiness not one smidge if our focus is on perfection. Enjoy the bliss of the moment you're in. Enjoy the process of knitting. Love your accomplishments. Own your imperfections.

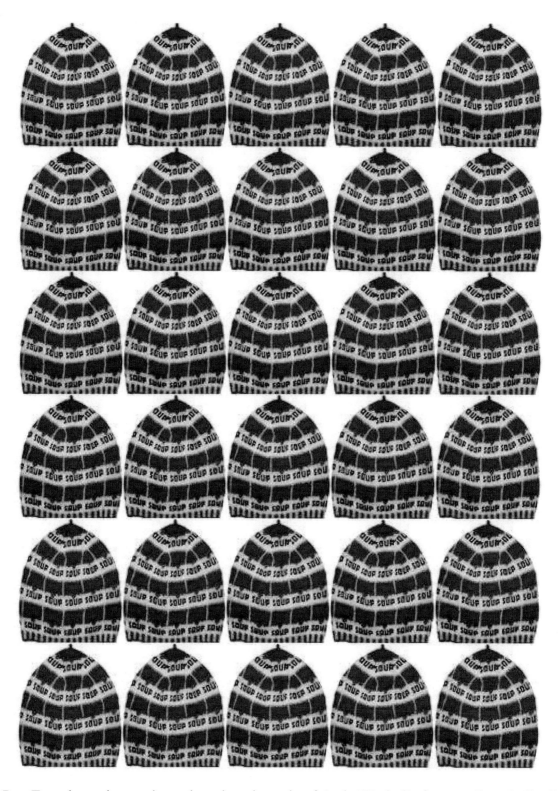

Pop Top, above, is my picture based on the style of Andy Warhol's famous *Campbell's Soup Cans*. Because of copyright law, I am not allowed to publish a photo of his original painting, which is on view at the Museum of Modern Art in New York. To see Warhol's work, visit here: http://www.moma.org/collection/object.php?object_id=79809

Pop Art

If you're not trying to be real, you don't have to get it right. That's art.
—Andy Warhol

Pop Art is a movement that evolved in the middle of the 20th century. Its focus on popular culture was an answer to the traditional fine art subjects that were in vogue up to that point. The movement was born from an attitude of subtle rebellion against personal, soft-edged abstract art. Pop Art, with its emotionally distant, edgy approach toward realism, took its topics from commercial advertising, popular culture, and current news events. It removed these items from their contextual settings, and made statements that were considered kitschy, ironic and mechanical.

One of the most widely known and instantly recognizable Pop artists is Andy Warhol (1928–1987). Interestingly, it is Warhol who is credited with coining the phrase "15 minutes of fame."[*] He was doing a publicity photo shoot, and passers-by were all trying to get into the photograph, Warhol commented that everyone wanted to be famous. His photographer then added (says he) "Yeah, for about 15 minutes, Andy." Although there is some controversy about which man actually originated the expression it is, indeed, Warhol who is credited with coining the well-known phrase. Warhol has many, highly valued and priceless pieces. One of the most enduringly popular of his works is *Campbell's Soup Cans* on view at MoMA.

This is the piece that inspired my *Pop Top* stranded hat. It is instantly recognizable as an adaptation of Warhol's genius work. As a tip of my hat to Mr. Warhol, I give you *Pop Top*.

[*] Guinn, Jeff and Douglas Perry (2005). *The Sixteenth Minute: Life In the Aftermath of Fame*. New York, Jeremy F. Tarcher/Penguin (a member of The Penguin Group). ISBN 0739455427. Guinn and Perry, pp. 36

P☐P T☐P.

Modeled by Natascha

Size: Child 6–10 years old

      Adult or Teen (21"–23" head circumference)

Materials: 1 ball each of Knit Picks Palette: *Tomato, Black, White,* plus small amounts of *Silver* and *Brass Heather*

      One 16" #3 circular needle, four #3 DPNs (or size needed to obtain gauge)

      Stitch marker

      Tapestry needle

Gauge: 32 stitches and 30 rounds = 4" using #3 needles.

NOTE: Use my unique Frequent Floats technique to create a hat whose inside is as smooth as its outside. I demonstrate in this YouTube video: http://www.youtube.com/watch?v=iYxX7MrpJ-Qs

Instructions: With circular needle, CO 136 sts using *Tomato.* Join to work in round, placing stitch marker and being careful not to twist stitches. Knit six rounds corrugated rib (see CHART A) using *White* for knit sts and *Tomato* for purl sts.

Increase Round: For adult hat only, increase 34 sts around evenly, every 4th st (K4, M1 in 4th st) for a total of 170 sts.

Follow CHART B (4 repeats per round for child hat—5 for adult hat) for 79 rounds, decreasing as indicated and switching to DPNs when necessary. (Each dec round has 2 decreases next to each other; k2TOG for first dec at beginning of chart, and SSK for second dec at end of chart each time.) After round 79, with 8 sts (10 for adult) on the needles, k2TOG around. 4(5) sts remain. Knit last 4 (5)sts for five rounds. Cut yarn leaving a tail several inches long. Move all sts from needles to tapestry needle, and pull tightly. Secure from the inside.

Finishing: Tie and weave in or trim all color change ends. Wash and block to fit.

CHART A

Use *White* for knit sts and *Tomato* for purl sts.
Dash in square = purl st

	4	3	2	1	
	—	—			6
	—	—			5
	—	—			4
	—	—			3
	—	—			2
	—	—			1

CHART B

23

Time Tam, above, is my picture based on Salvador Dalí's well-known surrealist painting *The Persistence of Memory*. Because of copyright law, I am not allowed to publish a photo of his original work, which is on view at the Museum of Modern Art in New York. To see Dalí's painting, visit here: http://www.moma.org/collection/object.php?object_id=79018

Surrealism

Drawing is the honesty of the art.
There is no possibility of cheating.
It is either good or bad.
—Salvador Dalí

Surrealism is an art movement evolving out of Dada. Dada was an art movement that formed in response to the evils of WWI. The Dadaists felt that the strict modernist rationality of thought was a cause for the Great War, and they rebelled by focusing on nonsense and irrationality rather than logic. Surrealism came to be in the 1920s and 30s. Picking up where the Dadaists left off, adding psychology and the force of the individual unconscious to round out the meaning of truth. Freud greatly influenced the thinking of the time, and surrealist artists, like Dalí, expressed the important element of the unconscious, blending dream-state visuals, non-contextual real-life items, and the imagination experienced in dreams. The movement influenced not only the visual arts, but also film, literature, poetry, theater, theories and design.

Salvador Dalí (1904–1989) was a filmographer, sculptor and photographer. He was also a great surrealist painter. In fact, he said that he himself *was* surrealism. Dalí was known for his publicity "stunts." For example, he appeared in commercials and *What's My Line*, a popular television show in the mid-20th century. But history has determined these "stunts" were actually performance art, rather than an outrageous display of shameless self-promotion. His best-known work is *The Persistence of Memory* (1931). The painting with its melting clocks is well known by most everyone, and it is the piece that directly influenced my *Time Tam*.

TIME TAM©

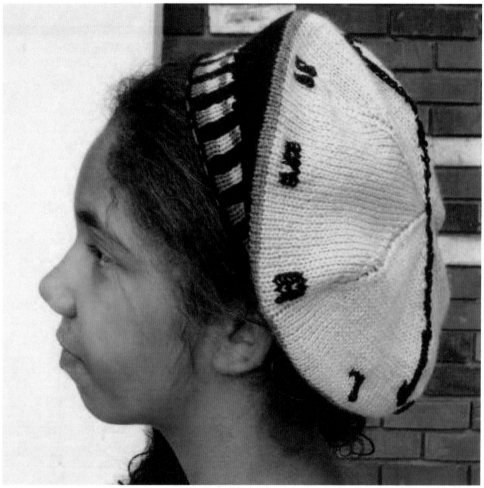

Modeled by Corrina

Size: Fits most adult heads 21"–23" in circumference

Materials: 1 ball each of Knit Picks Palette: *Whirlpool, Brass Heather,* and *Black,*
plus small amounts of *Masala, Caper,* and *Custard*

One 16" #2 circular needle

Four #2 DPNs

Stitch markers

Tapestry needle

Gauge: 34 stitches and 30 rounds = 4" using #2 needles.

Instructions: With circular needle, CO 144 sts using *Black.* Join to work in round, placing marker and taking care not to twist stitches. Knit 13 rounds corrugated rib (see chart A) using *Masala, Brass heather, Whirlpool, Caper* and *Custard* for knit sts and *Black* for purl sts.

Increase round: Using *Black*, inc evenly (M1 in every third stitch) around to192 sts.

Knit 16 rounds with *Black*.
Knit 3 rounds with *Brass Heather*.
Knit 16 rounds in *Whirlpool*.

Follow CHART B, placing markers after each 32 stitches (6 repeats per round) decreasing as indicated and switching to DPNs when necessary. (Each dec round has 2 decreases next to each other; K2TOG for first dec, and SSK for second each time.) Once CHART B is completed, with 6 sts on the needles, cut yarn leaving a tail several inches long. Move all sts from needles to tapestry needle, and pull tightly. Secure from the inside.

Finishing: Tie and weave in or trim all color change ends. Wash and block over a large dinner plate to obtain floppy tam shape.

Duplicate stitch in clock numbers (See CHART C) and embroider clock hands as shown in picture.

CHART A

Use *Masala, Brass heather, Whirlpool, Caper* and *Custard* for knit sts and *Black* for purl sts.
Purl black squares

	4	3	2	1	
					13
					12
					11
					10
					9
					8
					7
					6
					5
					4
					3
					2
					1

CHART B

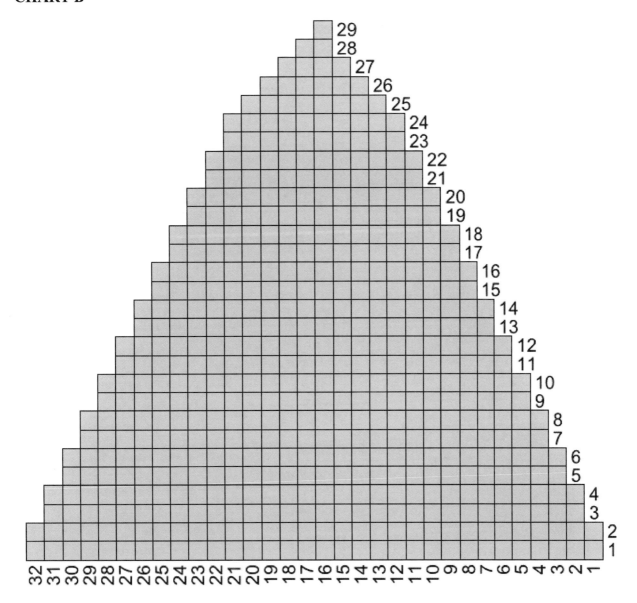

CHART C

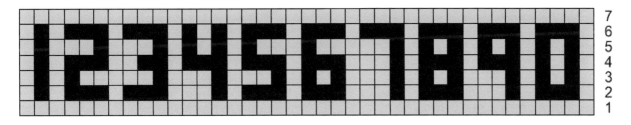

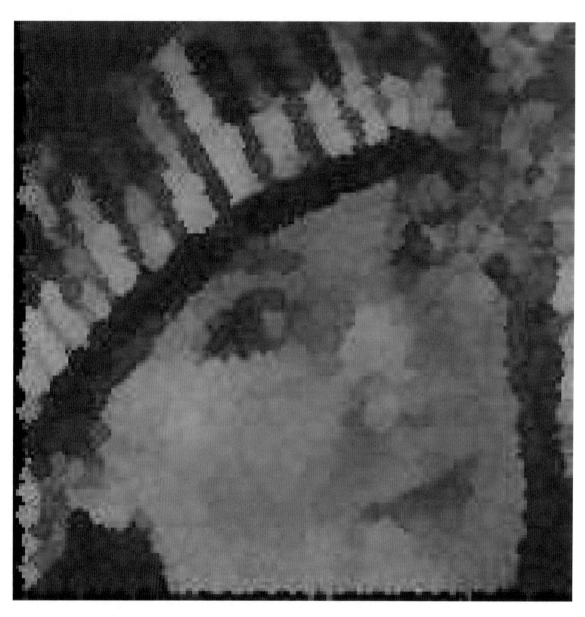

Musica Me, above, is my picture imitating the Pointillism style of using dots, or points of color, rather than brush strokes to create the overall effect. Georges-Pierre Seurat's famous *A Sunday Afternoon on the Island of La Grande Jatte* influenced my *Pointillism* shawl design and pattern. Because of copyright infringement law, I am not allowed to publish a photo of this great painting. The Art Institute of Chicago houses Seurat's piece.
http://www.artic.edu/aic/collections/artwork/27992?search_no=1&index=1

Pointillism

Some say they see poetry in my paintings; I see only science.
—Georges Seurat

Pointillism: Technically, I am cheating a little by including Pointillism with 20th-century art movements. It really began late in the 19th century, and it was developed by the famed painters Georges-Pierre Seurat and Paul Signac. The term Pointillism was coined as a negative critique of the style, which used individual dots of specific color arranged to create an image. This style was radically different from the traditional blending of colors on the artist's palette. In order to perceive the image the painter intended to convey, the viewer's eye and brain blend, or combine, the dots forming recognizable patterns and shapes.

I excuse my delving into the earlier century, recognizing that art forms rarely can be confined or defined by exact calendar dates. Alas, the Pointillism movement bled into the 20th century and moved over to music as a medium as well. Twentieth-century artists continued to use the technique.

Pointillism: The shawl uses individual stitches of color in lieu of the painter's dots. The overall mood conveyed is a blurring of the color changes. A beautiful blended fabric emerges, as can be seen in the shawl below.

POINTILLISM: The Shawl©

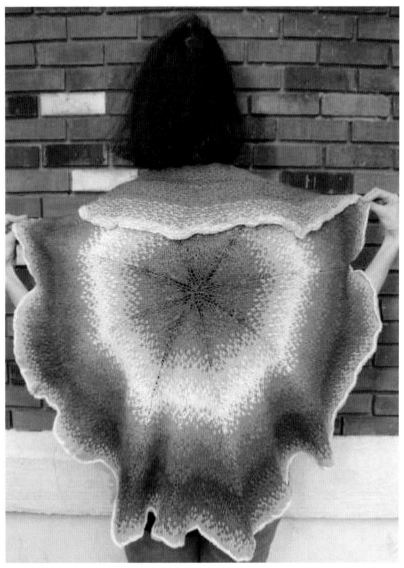

Modeled by Rena

Size: TBD by Knitter (at least 45" diameter)

Materials: 1 50g ball each of Knit Picks Palette: *Teal, Seafaring. Sagebrush, Mist, Pool,* and *Blue*

One multi-length cable #9 circular needle

Five #9 DPNs

Stitch markers

Tapestry needle

Instructions: Using two DPNs, and leaving a long tail for sewing later, CO 4 sts with *Teal*. Turn.

K1, M1 for 8 sts total. Turn.

Purl 8 sts. Turn.

K1, M1 for 16 sts total. Turn.

Purl 16 sts. turn.

K1, (K1, M1) for 24 sts total. Split sts evenly on 4 DPNs, 6 sts on each needle. Continue to work, from here on, in the round. (You will sew opening closed later.)

IMPORTANT: Float evenly and loosely every two stitches for a neat-looking shawl back.

Beginning with round two, work CHART A as follows: PM, K one chart repeat, PM around (8 chart repeats per round. 8 markers placed.) Add second color on round 5. When you have increased enough sts to warrant it, move work from DPNs to short circular, and switch to longer cable lengths as needed throughout. Knit through round 80. BO loosely on next round, using *Sagebrush*.

Finishing: With tail from CO, sew closed small slit left at the beginning when knitting the first few rounds. Tie and weave in or trim all color change ends. Wash and block flat.

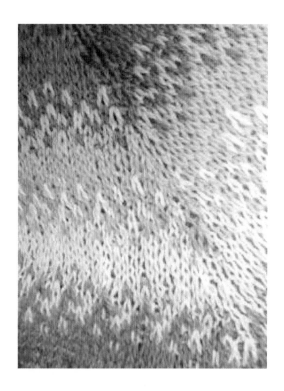

NOTE: On round 57, knit 3 sts in center st (and add marker) of each repeat as shown.

CHART A

Center square on round 56: place marker.

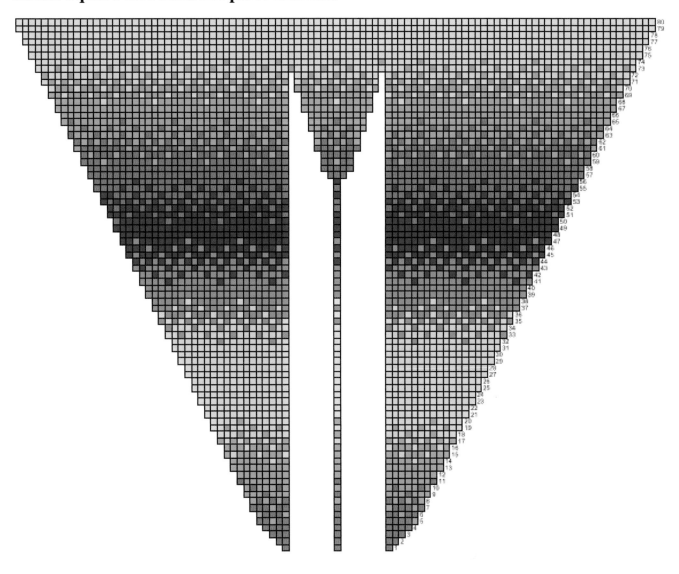

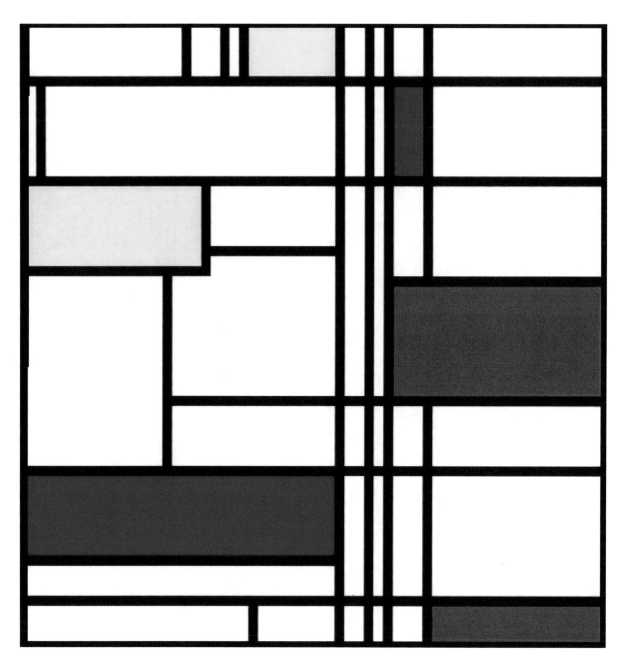

Mondrianesque, above, is a picture of my sweater design based on Piet Mondrian's famous work during the De Stijl movement. He referred to his unique style as "Neo-Plasticism." Because of copyright law, I am not allowed to publish a photo of his original work, which is on view at the Museum of Modern Art in New York. To see Mondrian's *Composition in Red, Blue and Yellow*, visit here: http://www.moma.org/collection/object.php?object_id=80160

De Stijl

In art the search for a content which is collectively
understandable is false;
the content will always be individual.

—Piet Mondrian

De Stijl, Dutch for "the style," began in Amsterdam in 1917. The movement was most popular in the first quarter of the 20th century. Its philosophy is referred to as neoplasticism, meaning the new plastic. It promotes the idea of utter simplicity and abstraction, and it reduces the use of color to the essentials: red, blue, yellow, black and white. Likewise, De Stijl advocates simplicity of form. The construction is basic and elemental; employing only vertical and horizontal lines.

As with all things, De Stijl didn't exist in a vacuum but was influenced by previous movements such as Cubism and Mysticism (purporting ideas of ideal geometric shapes). Furthermore, De Stijl ultimately gave rise to subsequent movements like Bauhaus, and it influenced styles in architecture and interior design.

Mondrianesque©

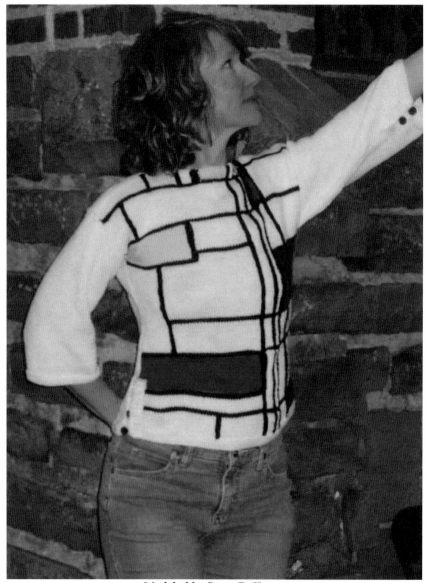

Modeled by Stacy DeYoung

Piet Mondrian, a 20th-century Dutch painter, evolved a nonrepresentational form of art he called Neoplasticism. His work comprised grids of horizontal and vertical black lines on a white background with blocks of the three primary colors: red, yellow, and blue. One of his most recognized pieces, a slight deviation from the above description, is *Broadway Boogie Woogie*. My *Mondrianesque* sweater captures the spirit of Mondrian's Neoplasticism ideas. It employs the intarsia technique of colorwork. Featuring a boat neck, tunic-style body and drop, ¾-length sleeves, it is a stunning, timeless treasure, suitable for all ages and sizes.

Sizes: Small (Medium, large)

Knitted Measurements: Bust 38"(40", 44") 97cm(101cm, 111cm)

Materials: Knit Picks Stroll Sport Yarn (75% Superwash Merino 25% nylon—137
yds per skein)

10 balls *White*

3 balls *Black*

1 ball *Winter Night*

1 ball *Hollyberry*

1 ball Knit Picks Swish DK (100% Superwash Merino) *Honey*

#6 needles (or size needed to obtain gauge)

Tapestry needle

12 buttons: Four each of red, blue, yellow to match yarn

Size F crochet hook for button loops

Gauge: 18 sts = 4" using #6 needles

Instructions for back: Using *White*, CO 90 (98, 118) stitches. K first row through
back loop. K garter for 1 inch. Turn. K 6 sts, purl across (stockinette) to last 6 sts,
K6 sts. Continue stockinette with 6-st garter edge on each side until back measures
4 inches from beginning. Then, continue back in all stockinette WITHOUT garter
edges until piece measures 23 inches total. BO.

Sleeves: Make 2. Using *White*, CO 72 (77, 81) stitches. K first row through back
loop. K garter for 1 inch. Turn. K 6 sts, purl across (stockinette) to last 6 sts, K6
sts. Continue stockinette with 6-st garter edge on each side until back measures 4
inches from beginning. Then, continue sleeve in all stockinette WITHOUT garter
edges until piece measures 13 inches (or desired sleeve length) total. BO.

Each stitch square on the chart represents 2 stitches and 2 rows. So, for each square, knit stitch twice and knit that row twice. When following the chart, purl back the chart row just knitted. Purl rows are not shown on chart.

Front: Using *White*, CO 90 (98, 118) stitches. K first row through back loop. K garter for 1 inch. Turn. Now knitting intarsia, begin following CHART A. For all sweater sizes, knit white-background sts. For Medium size, add block of sts shown in pink on chart: 8 stitches to pattern: 4 on one side and 4 on the other. For large, add both blocks of sts shown as pink and green on chart: 28stitches: 14 on one side and 14 on the other. BECAUSE EACH SQUARE IN THE CHART REPRESENTS 2 STS, chart shows half the number required. Follow appropriate breaks in chart for your size.

Work until front matches back in length. BO.

Construction and finishing: Wet block pieces. Machine st or carefully hand stitch shoulder seams one inch deep. Leave desired, neck-opening width. Turn under one inch and, with *White*, hem st under to complete neck. Hand sew sleeves to armhole openings, leaving garter placket open. Sew side seams, leaving garter plackets open. Tie in all yarn ends. Attach buttons. As seen in photo below.

Button loops: On other side, corresponding to buttons, crochet button loops, slip st the width of the placket, chain 10, attach and slip stitch back down the placket to form loop. Tie and weave in ends.

CHART A

Each stitch square on the chart represents 2 stitches and 2 rows. So, for each square, knit stitch twice and knit that row once and purl back equaling the 2 rows.

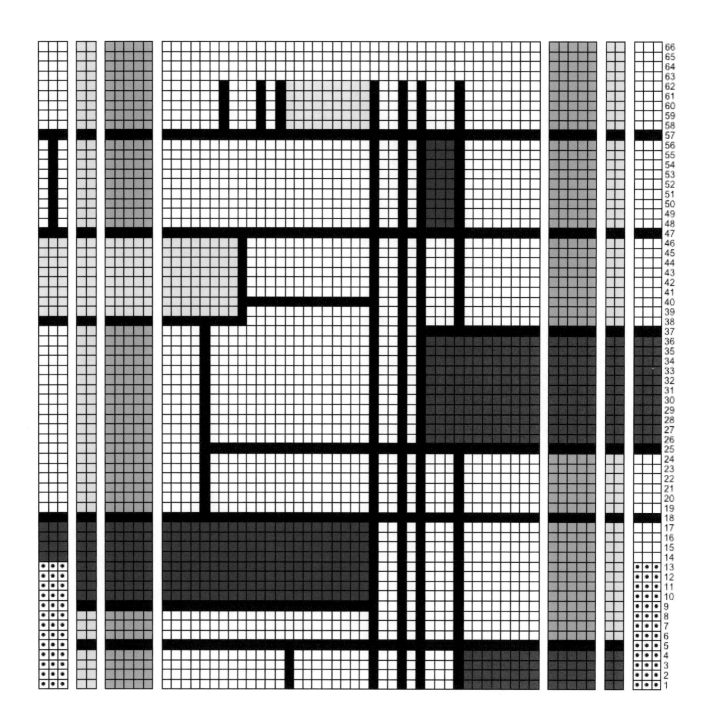

Cubist Ideas, above, is my picture pointing to the Cubism art movement. Because of copyright law, I am not allowed to publish photos of actual Cubist painting But you can view many of Pablo Picasso's famous Cubism pieces at MoMA. See *The Three Musicians*, which inspired my piece, here: http://www.moma.org/collection/object.php?object_id=78630

Cubism

The purpose of art is washing the dust of
daily life off our souls.
—Pablo Picasso

Cubism: Pablo Picasso, along with Georges Braque, founded this highly influential art movement during the first decade of the 20th century. As with all defined art movements, Cubism was set in motion by, and evolved out of, earlier styles. Paul Cézanne's style of representing three-dimensional forms in his late works was a primary influence of the Cubism movement. Cubist painters took real-life objects, analyzed the parts, broke them up, and then constructed them in abstract forms on canvas. Cubist paintings were not concerned with three-dimensional, realistic representations of their subjects. Rather, objects were depicted on a single, flat plane, with all "faces," or surfaces, simultaneously visible.

Historically, the term "Cubism" seems to have derived from Matisse's description of the elements of a 1907 Braque painting as "cubes."

Remembering Cubism: The Felted Bag©

Photo by Petra Vatne

Size: TBD by knitter: Cover Project measures 4"x 10" x 11" after felting

Materials: 5 balls Knit Picks Wool of the Andes *Coal (Must use wool that will felt well)*

One 10.5 or 11 29" circular needle

7-mesh plastic canvas or cross-stitch canvas, optional

Small amounts of worsted gray, brown, beige, white, flesh-tone, black, rose and purple for front design

Stitch Marker

Tapestry needle

Gauge: Gauge is not important here.

Instructions: CO 45 sts, using worsted yarn DOUBLED. Work back and forth in garter st 25 rows. This will be the bottom of the bag.

Now, rather than turn to knit back, continue around, picking up and knitting 25 sts down the short side, turn 90 degrees, pick up and knit 45 CO sts, turn 90 degrees and pick up and knit the 25 sts on the last short side. Place marker for round beginning here. 140 sts total.

From this point on, you will be knitting with 2 strands, in the round, on 140 sts.

Using two strands of yarn as if you are doing colorwork, continue to knit for 64 rounds (approx. 15" tall). Be sure to float *every stitch*…you want a nice, tight-looking backside with no long floats...not even 2 sts. See my easy technique for frequent floats here: http://www.youtube.com/watch?v=iYxX7MrpJ-Q

For handles: Round 65: K12, BO21, K49, BO21 K37. This will only work if you have 140 sts.
Round 66: K12, CO21, K49, CO21, K37.

K 8–10 more rounds. BO loosely.

Felt.

Work CHART A either by embroidering onto the felted bag directly, cross stitching on 7-mesh canvas, or working needlepoint on 7-mesh plastic canvas as I did in the cover bag.

Finishing: If working Cubism design separately from bag, sew canvas with finished work onto the front of the felted bag.

Shoulder strap option courtesy of Thiagram on Ravelry (Thank you, Cynthia!)

Using a single strand of yarn cast on 90 stitches.

Using a double strand of yarn K 4 rows

K5, BO4, K72, BO4, K5 (Measure button to stitches and cast off accordingly. Or, button can be sewn on without buttonhole if desired.)

K5, CO4, K72, CO4, K5

K4 rows

BO with a single yarn and a larger needle to ensure a loose bind off

CHART A

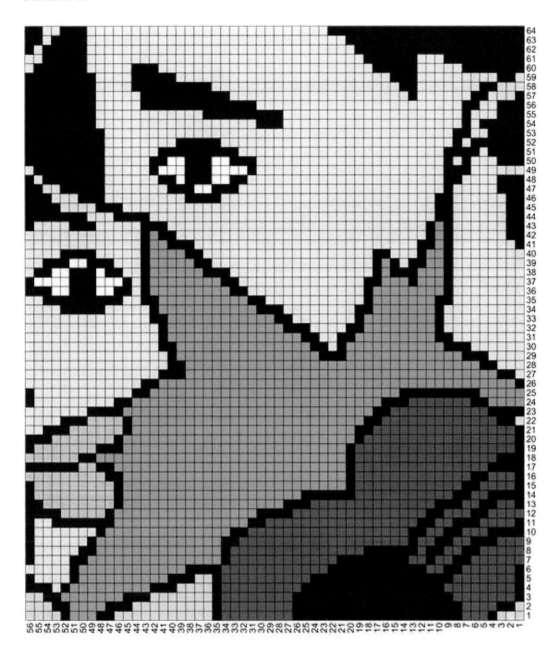

Homage to Albers, above, is my picture imitating Josef Albers's *Homage to the Square: With Rays*. Because of copyright law, I am not allowed to publish a photo of this Post-Painterly Abstraction painting. But you can view it here: http://www.metmuseum.org/toah/works-of-art/59.160

Post-Painterly Abstraction

Learn to *see* and to *feel* life, cultivate imagination,
because there are still marvels in the world, because life is a
mystery and always will be. But *be aware of it.* . . Art means:
you have to believe, to have faith, that is, to cultivate vision.

—Josef Albers

Post-Painterly Abstraction is actually the name given to an art exhibit curated by art critic Clement Greenberg in 1964. Greenberg saw a new movement evolving out of Abstract Expressionism; a movement favoring "openness and clarity" * over the densely painted surfaces of the former style.

Post-Painterly Abstraction gained a short-lived foothold in the 1960s, but it was replaced by subsequent movements like minimalism, hard-edge painting, lyrical abstraction and color field painting.**

* http://www.sharecom.ca/greenberg/ppaessay.html
**http://en.wikipedia.org/wiki/Post-painterly_abstraction

Josef Albers (1888–1976) was an artist and educator whose work formed the basis for some of the most influential art-related education programs of the 20th century. German-born Albers is probably most well known for his series of oil paintings on Masonite entitled *Homage to the Square*. The hat, like Albers's paintings, features colorful, nested squares that virtually pop out at you.

H☐mage t☐ the Square©

Modeled by Stacy DeYoung with Kipling

I designed this stranded colorwork pattern in honor of German-born American artist Josef Albers (1888–1976). Because this is knitted with three strands of wool per round, it works up into an extra cushy, warm fabric. The pattern features short repeats, so the chart is easy to follow. And, because it's knit in the round, it employs only the knit stitch. No purls. Nothing fancy-schmancy. The beauty is created simply, and nearly exclusively, through use of color. It's so much fun to knit and watch the squares appear as you go!

Size: One size fits average-to-large adult head

   Finished size when blocked: approx..21" – 23"

Materials: 1 ball each of Knit Picks Palette: *Celestial* (Color A), *Limeade Heather,* and *Cyan*

   One 16" #4 circular needle, four #4 DPNs (or size needed to obtain gauge)

   Stitch marker

   Tapestry needle

Suggested materials: One ball each of yarns listed above, or any three coordinating and/or contrasting Knit Picks Palette (100% Peruvian Highland wool 231yds per 50-gram ball). Or, one ball each of any three coordinating and/or contrasting Cascade 220 Fingering wool (100% Peruvian highland wool 273 yards per 50-gram ball).

Gauge: 30 stitches/ 21 rounds = 4" in stockinette stitch using #4 circular needle

NOTE: Remember that tension is crucial when doing stranded colorwork. Keep tension loose and consistent, remembering to float yarns on the back if they are carried for five or more stitches. Not every round in this pattern requires floats, but on the rounds where you do need to create floats, you will be carrying the *two* unused strands, rather only one strand as is typical in most colorwork.

Instructions: With circular needle, CO 136 sts using *Celestial* (Color A). Join to work in round, placing stitch marker and being careful not to twist stitches. Knit six rounds corrugated rib (see CHART A) using *Cyan* and *Limeade Heather* for knit sts and *Celestial* (Color A) for purl sts.

Increase round: (Round 1 of CHART B) Using *Celestial* (Color A), inc evenly to 165 sts: Knit 12, (knit 4, M1) around to last 8 sts. Knit last 8 sts.

Follow CHART B (11 repeats per round) for 61 rounds, decreasing as indicated and switching to DPNs when necessary. NOTE: Each dec round has 2 decreases next to each other; K2TOG for first dec, and SSK for second each time. After round 61, with 11 sts on the needles, K1, then K2TOG around. Six sts remain. Knit last six sts for five rounds. Cut yarn leaving a tail several inches long. Move all sts from needles to tapestry needle, and pull tightly. Secure from the inside.

Finishing: Tie and weave in or trim all color change ends. Wash and block to fit.

CHART A

Use *Limeade Heather* and *Cyan* for knit sts and *Celestial **(Color A)*** for purl sts. Dash in st means purl

4	3	2	1	
	—	—		6
	—	—		5
	—	—		4
	—	—		3
	—	—		2
	—	—		1

CHART B

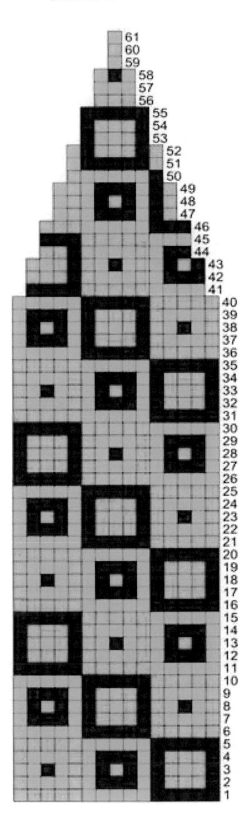

Trippin' Butterflies, above, is a picture exemplifying the psychedelic art movement of the 1960s.

Psychedelic Art

Through all of history mankind has ingested psychedelic substances.
Those substances exist to put you in touch with the spirits
beyond yourself, with the creator,
with the creative impulse of the planet.

—Ray Manzarek

Psychedelic art isn't generally recognized as a movement in its own right. It refers to any art that was inspired by psychedelic experiences like those rising from the use of LSD, mescaline or psilocybin. This places its popularity of style firmly in the 1960s, when usage of these drugs was ubiquitous. "Psychedelic" means "mind manifesting," and the artistic results of a painter's effort to convey the goings-on of the inner mind are thus called psychedelic art. In fact, psychedelic artists claimed that the altered states of consciousness, brought about by imbibing the psychedelic drug of choice, was the source of artistic inspiration.

Psychedelic art became popular with commercial designers, as well as the general public. It was used in posters and album covers, and hippies painted it on their vans and VW Beetles.

The swirling patterns of LSD hallucinations and the vivid, vibrant colors experienced therein can be seen and recognized in psychedelic art. The 1960s was a chaotic decade in the United States. The political unrest and outspoken voices of the counterculture have become a part of historical record, and these sentiments have been forever captured in the art of the time.

 **The Socks** ©

Modeled by "Monbeam"

Featuring Cat Bordhi's *Sweet Tomato Heel*

Size: Women's Medium-Large

Materials: 1 ball each of Knit Picks Palette colors: *Majestic, Cosmopolitan, French Lavender, Cyan, Celestial, Limeade Heather, Macaw, Canary, Kumquat Heather, Orange,* and *Tomato**

* For a pair of socks, you will only need small amounts of each color beyond *Majestic.*

> One long circular needle, two circular needles, or 5 DPNs, size#2 and #3 or size needed to get the correct gauge working in the round
>
> Two stitch markers
>
> Tapestry needle
>
> Nylon thread to reinforce heels and toes, if desired.

Gauge: 32 stitches and 30 rounds = 4"

Instructions: Socks are worked top-down.

Leg: With #2 circular needle or DPNs, CO 64 sts using *Majestic* (16 sts on each of 4 DPNs). Join to work in round, placing marker and being careful not to twist stitches. Knit 12 rounds 2x2 rib.

Switch to #3 needle and follow CHART A (1 repeat per round), for a total of 55 rounds. Rearrange sts on round 55 as you go, setting up for the heel as follows: knit 16 sts on first needle plus 5 more from second needle. This gives you 21 sts on the first needle. Now, on next needle knit 11 stitches. On third needle, knit 11 stitches and move the last 5 sts to the 4th needle. Knit those 5 plus the 16 already on needle 4 for a total of 21 sts on needle 4.

Needle 1 has 21 sts
Needle 2 has 11 sts
Needle 3 has 11 sts

Needle 4 has 21 sts.

NOTE: Remember to create floats every 2 sts on socks so toes don't get caught when putting on the sock!

Heel: No more gussets! This pattern features Cat Bordhi's ingenious Sweet Tomato Heel (STH). Cat Bordhi developed her STH over many months, working closely with over a hundred test knitters of all skill levels. During this time she distilled her illustrations and explanations again and again, until her test knitters and tech editor agreed the instructions were as clear and perfect as possible. In order to be sure that her work is not misrepresented, Cat asks that designers who wish to use her heel in their patterns send their readers directly to her free videos as well as to purchasing links for her eBook, *Cat's Sweet Tomato Heel Socks* ($20), and to the eBook's individual patterns ($6 each). She is encouraged that many knitters have been able to work from the free videos alone; if not, the eBook or individual patterns will give you the detailed instructions, illustrations, and explanations you need.

Links: (Copy and paste into your web browser.)

Video: Sweet Tomato Heel: http://tinyurl.com/4x4xmp2
Video: Padded Sweet Tomato Heel: http://tinyurl.com/3dayxlt
To purchase eBook: http://catbordhi.com/books/cats-sweet-tomato-heel-socks-3/
To purchase individual patterns: http://catbordhi.com/category/patterns/socks/

Once you understand Cat Bordhi's STH, proceed with sock. Follow Cat Bordhi's heel instructions, knitting heel with #2 needles and *Majestic* and nylon thread, if desired. Work three wedges on the 42 sts. Work wedges leaving 8 stitch pairs on each side (10 heel sts left unpaired between pairs). Knit instep stitches on #3 needle using *Cosmopolitan.*

Foot: Working all sts on circular needle or split evenly on DPNs as with leg, 16 sts per needle, and using #3 needle, work CHART A through round 44.

Toe: Using *Cyan* and nylon thread, if desired, decrease for toe as follows:

Needle 1: K to last 3 sts of NEEDLE 1, K2TOG, K1
Needle 2: K 1, SSK, knit until the last 3 stitches of NEEDLE 3
Needle 3: K to last 3 sts, K2TOG, K1
Needle 4: K1, SSK knit to last 3 sts of NEEDLE 1

Repeat this until there are 7 sts left on each needle. Place sts from needles 4 and 1 onto one needle (14sts). Place sts from needles 2 and 3 onto another needle (14 sts).

Graft the remaining stitches together using Kitchener st, and weave in all ends.

Finishing: Tie and weave in or trim all color change ends at beginning and ends of rounds. Wash and block to fit.

CHART A

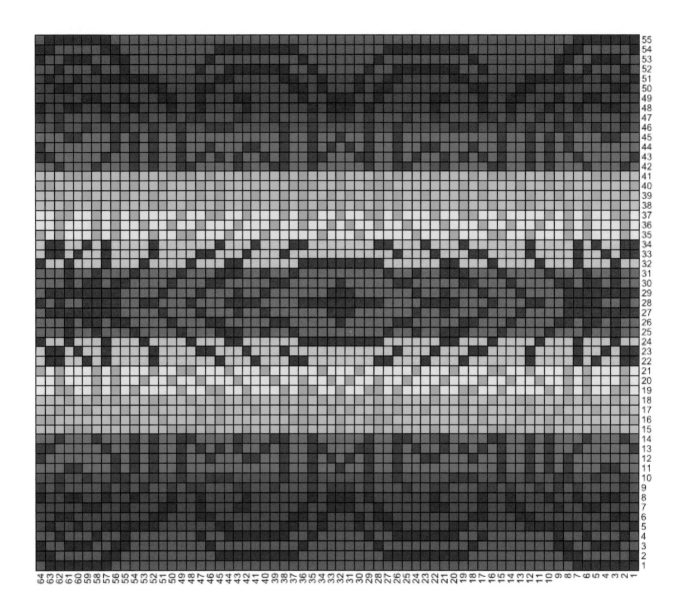

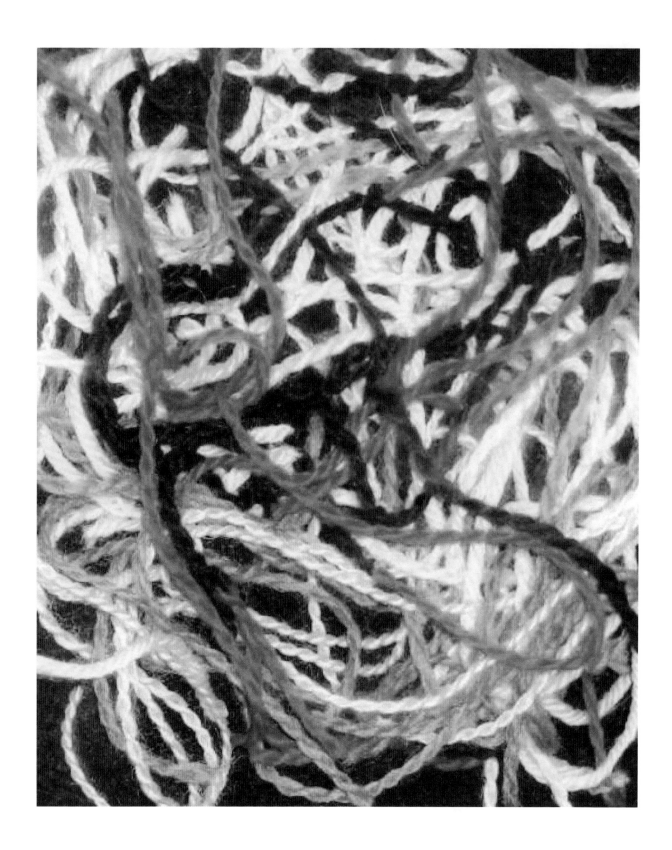

Abstract Expressionism

Today painters do not have to go to a subject matter
outside of themselves. Most modern painters work from
a different source. They work from within.

—Jackson Pollock

Abstract Expressionism is one of the first originally American art movements to gain worldwide importance. It was developed in New York in the 1940s and led to New York becoming a global art center, where Paris had been so formerly. The paintings of this movement are characterized by use of the entire canvas for painting, with no specific part of the canvas garnering center stage. This is different from other art styles where the middle of the canvas draws the eye and holds the center of interest.

The movement focused on the busy and the chaotic. The works were action-filled, abstract, and emotionally intense. One of the most well-known artists of the movement was Jackson Pollock. With their all-over fields of color, Pollock's drip paintings are among his most highly recognizable works. Rather than stand at an easel with brush in hand, Pollock spread his canvas on the floor, liberating him from constraint of motion. Pollock would dance rhythmically and splash, drip or otherwise place the paint as his subconscious dictated.

Autumn Rhythm: Fingerless Mitts©

One Size: Woman and Teen Medium

Materials: 2 50g balls (103 yds) of Debbie Bliss Milano *Willow*

       Five #7 DPNs

       Stitch marker

       Tapestry needle

Gauge: 14 stitches = 4" using #7 needles.

MITTS (MAKE TWO):

Mitt: With #7 DPNs, CO 28 stitches (sts) Knit 2x2 rib for cuff, 2.5 inches long or to desired cuff length .

Round 1: Knit one stitch, place marker. Knit 8 rounds.

Increase for thumb as follows:

To increase thumb:

Round 9: m1, k1, m1 in first st (3 sts now in first st). Slip marker. Continue to k sts as shown around

Round 10: knit around.

Round 11: m1, k3, m1. Slip marker. Continue to k sts as shown around.

Round 12: knit around.

Round 13: m1, k5, m1. Slip marker. Continue to k sts as shown around.

Round 14: knit around.

Round 15: m1, k7, m1. Slip marker. Continue to k sts as shown around.

Round 16: knit around.

Round 17: m1, k9, m1. Slip marker. Continue to k sts as shown around.

Round 18: knit around.

Round 19: Move 11 thumb sts to fifth DPN (or waste yarn) to be worked as thumb later. M1 st in next st so you will be working the original 28 sts. Knit for 1.5 inches.

Work 2x2 ribbing for 2 inches. BO loosely.

Thumb:

Pick up 1 stitch from body of mitt, knit 11sts on 5th DPN or waste yarn (split so you're working on 3 needles) for a total of 12 thumb sts. Join. Knit 2x2 rib for an inch or desired length. Bind off.

Finishing: Embellish on mitt back as desired. Use duplicate stitch or embroidery to create Abstract Expressionistic designs of your choosing. Tie and trim all yarn ends. Wear layered over gloves as shown or as is for easy texting!

Op Art 4-Sided Spiral Tunnel is an example of Op Art. Created by AnonMoos, as an SVG file. Thank you for allowing me to use your work. http://commons.wikimedia.org/wiki/File:Op-art-4-sided-spiral-tunnel.svg

Op Art

An artist's failures are as valuable as his successes…
by misjudging one thing he conforms something else,
even if at the time he does not know
what that something else is.

—Bridget Riley

Op art, short for "optical art," is a dynamic form of art that employs visual trickery. It came to life in the 1960s. The most highly recognizable pieces were painted in black and white, comprised lines and geometric shapes, and they convey the idea of movement. The eye perceives motion, and the brain sees what is not actually on the canvas. The paintings seem to vibrate, warp, flash, or otherwise "travel," but of course it is the viewer's brain doing all the moving.

Op art was dismissed by critics as a form in its own right, but it was popular with the general public. Op art images were used heavily in commercial work. It was, and continues to be, linked with perception theories in psychology.

The effect of op art is created when the viewer's brain tries to recognize patterns; the brain tries to organize the image as it contrasts with the background. A sense of motion is detected, though the painting itself does not move. It exploits after-images the brain creates as color receptors fatigue.

Bridget Riley is a well-known op artist. M. C. Escher, one of my favorites with his impossible realities and tessellations, can be included in the list, though he declined to classify himself as an op artist.

Delusions Op-Art Shawl©

Modeled by Rena

Size: TBD by Knitter (at least 46" across top and 20" down center back, after blocking)

Materials: 2 balls of Knit Picks Palette: *Black* (231 yds per 50g ball)

2 balls of Knit Picks Palette: *White* (231 yds per 50g ball)

One long #8 circular needle

Stitch markers

Instructions: With *Black*, CO 4 stitches. Turn.

K1, M1 4 times: 8 stitches. Turn.

Purl 8 sts. Turn.

K1, M1, 8 times; 16 sts. Turn.

Purl 16 sts. Turn.

Begin with round 1 of CHART: Attach *White*.*K1 *White*, K2 *Black*, K1 *White*. Place marker. Repeat from * 3 more times.

Chart represents one wedge of four. Repeat chart across 4 times per row, slipping marker between wedges..

Purl second row per chart, and every even-numbered row. When working an all-*White* row, float the *Black* so it is the proper position for beginning the next row.

Remember LEO when floating: Float Loosely, Evenly, and Often.

Finishing: Tie and weave in or trim all color change ends. Wash and block flat.

CHART

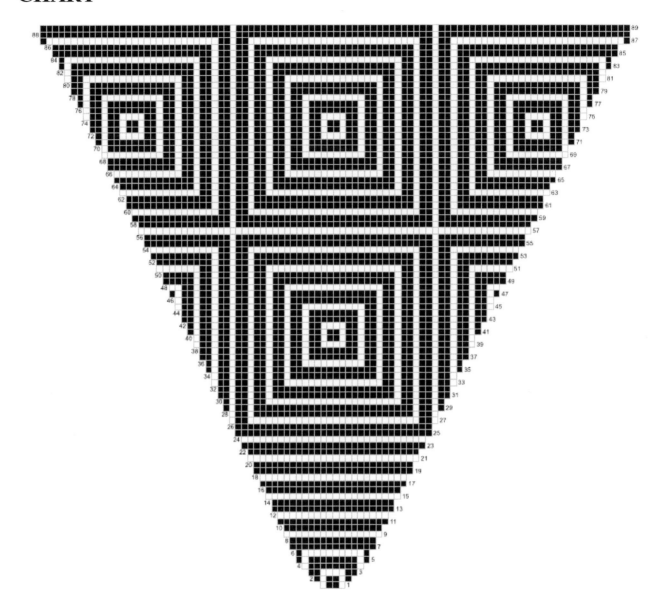

74

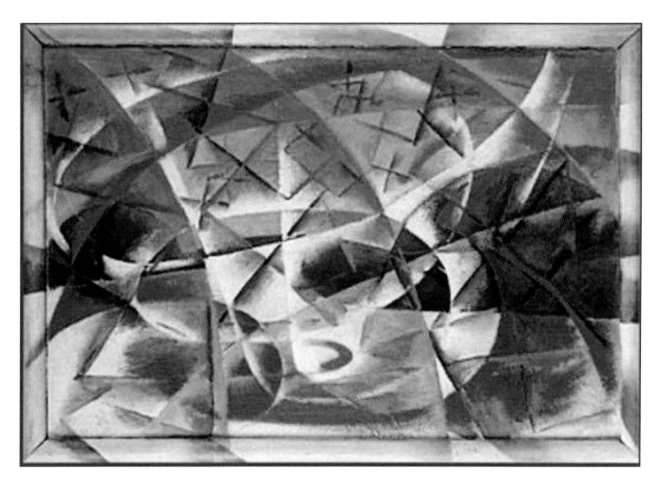

Giacomo Balla, *Abstract Speed + Sound* 1913–1914

Futursm

The gesture which we would reproduce on canvas shall no
longer be a fixed *moment* in universal dynamism.
It shall simply be the *dynamic sensation* itself.
—Technical manifesto of Futurist Painting

Futurism is an avant-garde art and social movement that was founded in Milan, Italy, in 1909. It centered its ideas on the then-modern ideas of what the future held. It concentrated on concepts of youth, violence and industrialized city life. It highlighted futuristic technologies of the day like high-speed modes of travel: cars and planes. It turned 180 degrees away from the past and concentrated on the future, as it was perceived before the fact.

Futurism celebrated man's ingenuity and invention over nature. The paintings were dynamic and energized, and they borrowed elements from Cubism, which can be clearly recognized in paintings like Giacomo Balla's *Abstract Speed + Sound,* shown above.

Futurism as a movement moved beyond painting. It embodied a social ideal, ventured into sculpture and architecture, and it spawned styles of musical composition, as well.

77

Approaching the SPEED of Light©

Modeled by Rena

Sizes: Approximately 7" x 62" after blocking

Materials: 2 balls Knit Picks Palette: *Black*

1 ball each Knit Picks Palette: *Tomato, Seafaring*, and *Bluebell*

One 29" circular #8 needle

Stitch markers

Tapestry needle

INSTRUCTIONS: Using provisional cast on, CO 240 sts with *Seafaring*. Place marker at the round beginning. Join, taking care not to twist sts. Begin knitting chart on round107. Knit it, and then knit round 108.

FOLLOW CHART Beginning with round 1, add one st. Knit 16 repeats per round, through round 54. On Round 55, K2TOG. Then continue to knit chart, 16 repeats per round through round 106. Detach *Black*. Cut *Seafaring*, leaving tail long enough to graft seam.

Graft last round and CO round together (not too tightly) using Kitchener st. See tutorial for Kitchener here:

http://www.youtube.com/watch?v=W7i5JwEReW0
Float loosely and evenly.

Finishing: Tie and trim all yarn ends. Soak and block vigorously. With the cowl in half, with the front design on one half and the back design on the other half. Make sure edges are straight and crisp.

CHART

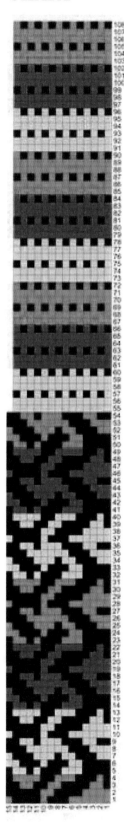

About the Author

Deborah Tomasello learned to knit and sew at her grandmother's knee when she was about five years old. Some of her fondest memories of her Gramma involve yarn and needles. She would start with grand ideas of knitting a scarf, but after working a few inches, when something of a lacy trapezoid would appear, she'd turn that scarf-gone-awry into a skirt for her Barbie. Over the years, her scarves became straighter, and her imagination broadened. Wools and fabrics have woven themselves into Deborah's very being, and she spends all her days happily designing and knitting her colorwork patterns.

Deborah has published several eBooks, *Stranded Knitting: It's Easier Than You Think, Four Strand Knitting: It's Easier Than You Think*, and *Stranded for Christmas*. She recently released her first book, *Wrapped in Color: Stranded Knitting in the 21st Century*. She has designed and published scores of colorwork patterns on Ravelry, Craftsy, Knit Picks and Patternfish. She has sold patterns to WEBs, and she won first place in Accord Publishing's 2014 Knitting Calendar for her *Brilliant Twilight* colorwork hat design.

Contact Information

Email Address: CoeDeborah@aol.com

Ravelry Group: http://www.ravelry.com/groups/colorworksbydebi-deborah-tomasello-designs

Made in the USA
Charleston, SC
05 June 2014